Wintertime Rhymes

Icy Delights

Edited By Jenni Harrison

First published in Great Britain in 2017 by:

Coltsfoot Drive
Peterborough
PE2 9BF
Telephone: 01733 890066
Website: www.youngwriters.co.uk

All Rights Reserved
Book Design by Ali Smith
© Copyright Contributors 2017
SB ISBN 978-1-78624-924-1
Printed and bound in the UK by BookPrintingUK
Website: www.bookprintinguk.com
YB0304V

Foreword

Dear Reader,

Welcome to Wintertime Rhymes, a showcase for our nation's most brilliant young poets to share what they love most about winter and the festive season. From poems about Christmas and snow to drinking hot chocolate in front of the fire, this collection covers every aspect of wintertime.

Young Writers was established in 1991 to nurture creativity in our children and young adults, to give them an interest in poetry and an outlet to express themselves. Seeing their work in print will encourage them to keep writing as they grow and become our poets of tomorrow.

Selecting the poems has been challenging and immensely rewarding. The effort and imagination invested by these young writers makes their poems a pleasure to enjoy reading time and time again. I hope you enjoy reading them as much as we did.

Jenni Harrison

Contents

Independent Entries

Aminah Rahman (13)	1
Rebekah Lane (10)	2
Lorna Beth Lee (16)	4
Jessica Nelson (12)	7
Layana Rose Sani (15)	8
Abbi Jane Sargeant (14)	10
Emma Jean Lilley (11)	12
Jessica Derrick (13)	14
Willow Bryant (14)	16
Trinity Belle Yoko Ota (13)	18
Ella-Rose Mulcare (15)	20
Jaskeerat Kaur Gill (13)	22
Nell Hodgson (13)	24
Zahra Tabarak (14)	26
Eleanor Howarth (14)	27
Alice Titley (14)	28
Zachary Green (16)	29
Indya Lilly Burke (11)	30
Molly Emery (15)	32
Lucy Matthews (14)	34
Xue Lin (11)	36
Anna Chudzik (12)	38
Holly Wolstenholme (15)	39
Azriel Bowles (15)	40
Maliha Hayyat (10)	42
Iqra Bibi (17)	43
Ruby Cline (13)	44
Megan Sutcliffe (18)	46
Satiya Bekelcha Yaya (15)	48
Deia Russell-Smith (17)	49
Mawadda Edbagi (12)	50
Hannah Duckworth (12)	52
Amin Edbagi (11)	54
Laurna Yeboah	56
Mawada Ben Taher (15)	57
Claudia Anton (12)	58
Megan Elizabeth Waite (10)	59
Jakir Ali (15)	60
Niamh Caroline Chalmers (11)	62
Saman Shahzad (14)	63
Lily Bennett (10)	64
Maggie Old-Gooch (13)	65
Thalia Warren (10)	66
Danny Joseph Byrne (11)	67
Imogen Barr (13)	68
Kewen Wang (13)	69
Tanica Cherelle Karen Anderson (13)	70
Nia Joseph (11)	71
Kaytie Alexander-Smith (13)	72
Toni Alice Crompton (13)	73
Maariyah Mumtahanah Syed	74
Virtudes Miralles (14)	75
Rosa-May Bown (14)	76
Grace Gbadamosi (14)	77
Freya Cerys Ashworth (12)	78
Nataliya Klymko (14)	79
Lucia Cyples (10)	80
Georgia Anne Ellis (12)	81
Isha Lamba (15)	82
Shannon Rose Byrne (15)	83
Niall Smith (10)	84
Chelsie Wheat (10)	85
Ruqaiyah Jarviton (12)	86
Fatimah Isap (10)	87
Laura Prentice (14)	88
Maariyaah Khan (13)	89
Natalie May Foster (10)	90
Keira Parker (15)	91
Tia Flanagan (14)	92

Anastasia Armstrong (12)	93
Chanice Esther Barrow (16)	94
Chantel Edwards (13)	95
Eve Newman (13)	96
Patricia Popa (14)	97
Jodie Stone (13)	98
Courtney Leigh (16)	99
Amy Stewart (14)	100
Tehillah Honny (12)	101
Atlanta Jade Revill (13)	102
Sinead Cheung	103
Maria Manta (11)	104
Georgie von Grundherr (14)	105
Zeinab Wnis (10)	106
Priyan Yaddehige	107
Todah Honny	108
Maizy Day (10)	109
Keira Harvey (10)	110
Shannon Clack (17)	111
Kira Mullen (10)	112
Usman Siddiqui (10)	113
Tayla Alison Schofield (13)	114
Hafsa Hussain (13)	115

Bathgate Academy, Bathgate

Jessica Jane Ross (14)	116
Elizabeth Snedden (14)	118

Cranbrook Education Campus, Exeter

Laura Williams (11)	119
Millie Downham-Elphick (11)	120

Harrogate Ladies' College, Harrogate

Sophie Berry (11)	121
Sophie McHugh (11)	122
Aimee Lauren Thomas (11)	123
Ella Teale (11)	124
Emily-Anne Jones (12)	125
Niamh Currie (12)	126

Cerys Young (11)	127
Hannah Grant (11)	128
Sofia Jarman (11)	129
Summer Elbortoukaly (11)	130

Holy Mary Catholic School, Madrid

Victoria Castro (12)	131

Lewes Old Grammar School, Lewes

Max Harrison (12)	133

Royds School, Leeds

Billy Adams (13)	135
Ben Russell (12)	136
Alfie Mortimer (13)	137
Zach Jones (12)	138
Callum Eric James Ibbotson (12)	139
Alfie McShane (12)	140
Aliesha Chamberlain (12)	141
Joe Dodworth (12)	142
Marshall George Fodden (12)	143
Katelyn Rowley (12)	144

St Illtyd's Catholic High School, Cardiff

Nicole Evans (12)	145

The Manor Academy, Mansfield

Holly Cooper (11)	146
Mia Green (11)	148
Emily Allden (15)	149

The Poems

Winter Is Here...

Winter is here; the soaring trees will stand bare,
Bonfire night takes place - hot chocolates and the winter fair.
Snowmen will rise and the icy winds will blow,
Going on frosty walks and having fun in the snow.
The mornings are dark and not a single sound is heard,
Not a footstep, a laugh; not even the tweet of a bird.
The delicate snowflakes descend from the midnight sky,
Christmas slowly arrives - presents, turkey and mince pie.
It's always cold; the sun rarely visits me,
You can just see a glimpse of her through the one naked tree.
The leaves are like cornflakes - so crunchy and brittle,
The snowflakes are so precious and little.
There is a time we should never forget, but to remember,
Bonfire night - the fifth of November.
Sparkling fireworks whizz up to the sky and burst with beautiful colour,
The bangs are extremely loud; at least it doesn't make the sky duller.
Winter is usually fun; a time to snuggle up with your family,
Get ready; it'll soon be time to put up the pretty Christmas tree.

Aminah Rahman (13)

Winter Spirit

On a biting Christmas Eve morning
When the blue sky turned a pale white,
And the soft delicate snowflakes fell
Onto the glistening surface,
Three children rushed outside into the frosty air
And began to make someone very special.

Heaving huge clumps of snow with teeth chattering
And wet hands, they created me! There I stood proud and tall.
My hands made of sticks from a nearby apple tree in their garden;
My hat and scarf carefully picked from their mother's wardrobe;
My three buttons and eyes made out of shiny black pebbles
And my huge carrot nose picked freshly from their garden.

I felt a tingling sensation run through my body
As the first snowflake touched my carrot nose.
My little stick fingers began to wiggle and jiggle
And I began to dance and sing to a merry tune.
My icy heart was full of life and joyfulness.
I was beaming happy and bright for this special day.

My carrot nose could smell the glorious festive dinners
And my ears made of frosty snow could hear the laughter
And music inside each home. I was alive!
I watched through a hole in the garden fence,
Children sliding around on sledges with delight
Screaming in excitement when it sped up.

All of a sudden a pebble slipped out of place
And then another, and another and another.
My hands felt droopy, my head was floppy and my face a mess.
I began to wonder what was happening; was I simply just tired?
I looked up to see something burning big and bright.
I heard someone shout, 'The sun's come out - let's play!'

When morning came, all that was left in sight
Was my little carrot nose, shiny pebbles and wet clothes
In a cold puddle which soon froze over.
I would have to wait for another chance
To bring my little stick hands to life again
I lay on the floor frozen still.
Waiting for a little drop of snow to fall once more.

I was the snowman with the winter spirit.

Rebekah Lane (10)

A Christmas Miracle

The day the air grew icy,
Was the day winter arrived,
The day the sky turned white with snow,
I knew autumn was left behind,

The frostbitten autumn leaves,
Trapped in their icy frame,
A mosaic of autumn colour,
I knew winter was to blame,

The first wet snowflake flurries,
Falling down, down, down,
Only to disappear,
Once they hit the ground,

It wasn't really snow,
More like icy rain,
I sat at my window disappointed,
Knowing it was never going to lay,

Wet puddles caught any snow that came,
Drowning them in its icy grip,
I sat at my window watching,
Hoping it would all be over quick,

I sat and watched all winter,
Wishing for it to be white,
I wished and wished for snow,
Every single night,

I knew it was all useless,
Winter had nearly passed,
I needed a Christmas miracle,
And I was going to need it fast,

Then on Christmas morning,
After wishing aloud all night,
I opened up my curtains,
And... 'Snow!' I cried with delight,

I ran outside in my nighty,
Not bothering to look under the tree,
My Christmas present was in the garden,
And it was waiting there for me,

I ran around in my snow,
I frolicked in it all day,
I wouldn't go back inside,
Scared it would all go away,

My parents explained to me,
That after all that sleet,
We were the only ones that caught the snow,
On the entire street,

I only found out recently,
About the snow machine,
That my parents used that day,
To make that snow for me.

Lorna Beth Lee (16)

Winter Time

Snow is falling down, our gardens are covered in frost,
Winter is now here, the sun and heat are lost.
Snowmen wearing scarves and hats, snow angels when children play,
Snowballs thrown from one another even though it's a cold and freezing day!
The trees look bare and frozen; they sway gently in the breeze.
People are using sledges, and snow boots and skis.
When December comes, the Christmas trees go up.
People buy the festive foods and even drink from Christmas cups.
Santa is in his sleigh, the reindeers are all ready,
Children get their presents, whether it's a doll or a toy
or a teddy.
Carols are sung and ice is skated on.
The Christmas bible story is told by Matthew, Mark, Luke and John.
Thick duvets are worn at night and evening fires are lit.
The nights pull in quicker and there are jumpers to buy
or knit.
When winter is over, the snow melting will begin.
Tree leaves will slowly grow back and in the sky,
The sun will find its way back in.

Jessica Nelson (12)

My Winter Wonderland

The wind bears ice - the rain hardens
The trees freeze and crystallize in mystical silence.
The animals hear it too; they feel it in their bones
They sense it like I do, and hurry into their homes.

It's here again, it's time -
Time to disappear into my winter wonderland.

The sky is heavy - brimming with magic
The wind hums a familiar tune, so simple yet enigmatic.
Slowly the skies crack open, scattering the stillness with crystals,
White diamonds from heaven, serenity's symbols.

A tiny snowflake cools my skin, holds my hand
And gently leads the way to my winter wonderland.

Now, strange men start to appear - men made of snow
Men with wonky pebbled smiles and a comic carrot nose
There's one then one hundred then one thousand; they quickly reproduce
Winter belongs to them; their population is so profuse.

These figures of ice - with cold bodies and warm hearts
Are the indigenous people of my winter wonderland.

Here, the rules don't apply, it's an eternal bliss
The Earth stops spinning and time itself freezes into an abyss.
Reality becomes fantasy as it hides in a blanket of white
This planet becomes a snow globe, hidden out of sight.

All you need is a head full of imagination
To live a little while in my winter wonderland.

We can make a snow angel or create an army of snowmen
We can have messy snowball fights, again and again
We can grab a sledge or skate across icy lakes
We can spend a lifetime here, if that's what it takes.

Would you like to join me,
In my winter wonderland?

Layana Rose Sani (15)

The Joys Of Christmas

20th of December
And the fire is burning amber
The streets are full of fog
But we sit by the fire drinking eggnog
The crisp of the early mornings
Dreading getting up when everyone is snoring
My toes are numbing
The birds are humming
The cold stings my cherry coloured lips
I hold my hot chocolate only taking little sips
It's time to go Christmas shopping
There's no time for stopping
Time to wear your gloves and hat
We ask for toys while sitting on Santa's lap
Pine coloured leaves turn golden brown
And Christmas has overtaken the town
People laugh with joy
We look in the windows trying to find the latest toy
When the day comes to an end
A Christmas letter is what we send
We sit in the warm watching the snow fall
We see the shining snowman standing up tall

The family is around
The Christmas carollers sing a beautiful sound
We decorate the tree
With the Christmas glee
It's Christmas eve
And Santa is ready to leave
It's 9 o'clock and we are in bed
We have to listen to what Mum said
We have to be asleep
We are not allowed to peep
Santa will sneak through
He puts the presents in our stockings too
He comes down the chimney without a sound
Carrying a sack that weighs more than a pound
But still
no sound.

Abbi Jane Sargeant (14)

Winter

Socks and boots and jackets and mittens,
frozen pink cheeks and baby kittens.
A puppy, a mother's warm hug, a father's great smile,
and a little sister's toys to trip on meanwhile.

Sitting by the fire, life could be no better,
a scarf and hat, a frozen baseball bat,
next to my frozen soccer ball,
stuck to the grass because of snowfall.

Sitting in the quiet drinking hot chocolate,
and reading a book as time slowly goes by.
A tick, a tock, the old grandfather clock gently marks the hour.

A dong, dong, dong, a bing, a bong, bong,
Time seems to stop, sweet memories it brings,
and the room is brightening with the sound of laughter
as Christmas crackers pop under the Christmas tree.

As summertime passes the old water glasses
slowly turn to mugs of coffee and tea.
Ice cream turns to gingerbread men and mince pies and pudding.

As the radio plays Christmas carols and I start to fall asleep.
Right now, there's no place else where I'd rather be,
than watching my snowman slowly start to freeze.

Emma Jean Lilley (11)

Winter For Me

Slowly, silently, secretly
White diamonds fall from the skies
Creating a magical world of white canvasses
Green lawns start to disappear
Underneath a thick white carpet
Spoilt by paw-prints of midnight visitors
Sparkling crystals dance in the air
Whirling and twirling as light as a feather
Cuddling trees with warm overcoats
And flowers in cosy hats
Cars transformed into fluffy cupcakes
Going nowhere
The world awakes
Morning moans turn to cheers
As schools are closed and parents home
Squish, squash wellies crush the crystals flat
Slip! A child falls onto the white cold blanket
Crunchy and cold like a slush puppy
Shovels crunching clearing the white powder
Armies of men start to appear
From small to tall, chubby to thin
All with orange triangular noses

Whee! Rosy red children sliding down hills
And imprinting angels with wings like fluffy clouds
While parents chit chat over hot cocoa
Drip drop... the enemy arrives
The poor snowman, there's nothing he can do
As he suddenly loses his power
Plop! He loses a limb
And starts to stoop
Quickly, slyly, cruelly
The magical white kingdom disappears
...Until next time

Jessica Derrick (13)

Winter Is...

Winter is when all the animals sleep,
Winter is when snowflakes float and land on your nose.
Winter is when you see all the Christmas presents in a heap,
And winter is how all the tree lights glow.

Winter is the cold morning sun,
Winter is the rough woollen scarf your grandma makes you wear.
Winter is when all you do is have fun,
And winter is Christmas morning when you hide on the stair.

Winter is the dark sky at night,
Winter is all the stockings hanging above the fireplace.
Winter is when the ground is white,
And winter is when a smile never leaves your face.

Winter is when your lips go numb,
Winter is when frost paints the car.
Winter is when you see that what's left on the plate is only a crumb,
And winter is when you want to see Santa so you leave the door slightly ajar.

Winter is a snowball fight,
Winter is when your family takes you on a freezing walk by the sea.
Winter is the story of how the snowman took flight,
But most of all, winter is whatever you wish your winter to be...

Willow Bryant (14)

The Joys Of Christmas Day!

The snow falls heavily on my house top,
Stealing all heat from inside,
But we don't notice the biting chill,
For 'It's Christmas!' we all cry.

Every family awake before 7,
Filled with Christmas love,
The kids wake up the parents,
To the sound of little toy doves.

And no breakfast is made that morning,
For the house is too busy to eat,
Only music and presents and Christmas TV,
And of course, some comforting heat.

And as the people sit down near their hearths,
Whether electric or not,
The atmosphere is laced with spirit,
And nobody is forgot.

When the time for presents is nigh,
We all crowd close together,
Excited at the prospect of new things,
We'll cherish and enjoy forever.

But after the presents are given,
Christmas is nowhere near,
Do we sit around fiddling with ribbon?
No, it's nearly New Year!

Trinity Belle Yoko Ota (13)

All I Want For Christmas...

Excitement fills the house so warm,
As Christmas is here the day Jesus Christ our Lord was born.
When I wake up I want to see presents in my stocking,
When lunch is ready I hope for a feast set for a king.

There's nothing better I could wish for,
Especially when Santa Claus slides down our chimney forever more.
His reindeer on the roof so high,
Flying into the moonlit sky.

Santa leaves presents under the tree,
A puppy in a box wrapped up for me.
For sister a new white telly,
And for dad used socks. Smelly!

When food is finally ready,
We all race to get the turkey.
Everyone leaves the veggie sprouts,
As the flavoured meat waters our mouths.

After tea Mum and Dad are off out,
It makes our grandmother pout.
Almost like cleaning up the sprouts,
It's Christmas day and all I want to do is scream and shout.

Board games played by an open fire,
Grandad never begins to tire.
And as the day ends we make next year's wish,
That's all I want for Christmas.

Ella-Rose Mulcare (15)

Winter Is The Warmest Season

You probably think I'm loony,
Winter, the warmest season?
Yeah that's right.
It's so easy to catch hypothermia.

No but I'm being serious,
Winter is the warmest season.
If you don't believe it yourself,
Read on to discover.

Picture this,
You're inside on the cosy sofa,
You have a bowl of popcorn and Home Alone is on.
Ahh... the bliss.
You're so cosy and warm.

Picture this,
You're wearing an oversized hoodie,
Wearing your favourite, fluffy unicorn socks.
You have a mug of hot chocolate,
You're so cosy and warm.

Picture this,
You've finally found the right temperature,
To turn to on the house heating.

Sit back on the sofa and recline,
Grab that blanket Nan made for you last Christmas.
You're so cosy and warm.

So now do you understand,
How winter is the warmest season?
From blankets to socks,
Hot chocolate to Christmas smocks,
Winter is officially the warmest season.
Though not climatically of course!

Jaskeerat Kaur Gill (13)

Peace In Wonderland

Desolation.
No one is here,
Peace and tranquillity,
No one to hear.

Misty cold morning,
Blue shrivelled hands,
8:22
8:25

Frosty and crunchy is the winter's curse,
Cold under the canopy,
The sun the winter's nurse.

Minty green grass,
Coupled with bliss blanket ignorance.

8:31
8:32
This moment will soon be over.

My ears nibbled by cold,
I fiddle with mittens,
With buttons shaped like kittens.

A girl strolls over the frost,
The cold budding ice wriggles and crunches,

She seems lost,
Lost within this foggy landscape,
Survival of the fittest.

I pack away pencil and notepad,
It is over,
This time of peace and tranquillity,
Trapped in a memory.

Inhabited.
Everyone is here,
Noise and chaos,
Everyone to hear...

Nell Hodgson (13)

Winter City

Long winding cobblestone paths
Covered in falling flakes of snow
Leafless trees with frost for skin
And their leaves stuck to the soil beneath
Frozen but never wilting flowers.

Shops which stay open through the night
Selling dreams and hopes for anyone lost
Buildings filled with people of all types
Their laughter floating down the streets
Cafes all offering cakes and all things sweet
And offering window seats of glowing stars

Cold nights which lead to lit fireplaces
Cups of hot chocolate with marshmallows
Warm entrapping hugs from loved ones
Story time as you huddle up listening intently
To tales of knights and princesses
Sleeping soundly afterwards in cosy beds

Such things take place in Winter City
A town of prosperity and all things right.
Winter is beauty despite her harsh habits.
Do not judge winter by her sudden coldness
For there is always warmth that follows by
Seeking forgiveness for everything winter's done.

Zahra Tabarak (14)

Christmas Tranquillity

The aged home, decorated with silver laced strings upon the doorway,
Accompanied by the mistletoe hung by a lonely ribbon,
Ruby-red as the flames bidden protectively behind the bricks of the abode
Crystals descending from the blanket above,
Gracefully resting upon the white layer of snow,
Surrounding everything in its icy embrace
The sky's glowing eyes and radiant glitter of vibrant, curtained lights,
Glistening down upon the beautiful, blissful peace of winter,
Unveiling the habitation of the wine-red breasted, feathered creatures atop the vaguely smouldering chimney,
Their small beaks faintly covered in the frozen, pearly substance,
The warm orange on their dear chest glowing proudly under the perfectly freezing shield of sleet
The tranquillity of Christmas,
Enveloping the small accommodation with a sheltering clasp,
Hoping to store and protect Christmas for evermore.

Eleanor Howarth (14)

Christmas Memories

Soon trees will stand bare,
Merciless ice winds will blast right through us.
Frosty morns and chilly nights, it will be a spectacular sight.
Nights away from the cold, winter's snow all snuggled
Up with warm hot chocolate that fills us with delight.
Christmas shopping with all the family waiting to celebrate the days of new coming.
Hustle and bustle in the streets checking off gift lists, even window shopping as your hands go numb.
Because you want everything done and to retire to a nice family night in.
Mass to go to, relaxing in the night remembering the experiences of the year.
Waiting again under the mistletoe, awaiting for your dreams to come true once more.
All will be done with and a new year will begin
With a joyful song of Auld Lang Syne with a cup of good cheer.
Christmas come again soon!
Merry Christmas to everyone.

Alice Titley (14)

A Gelid Panorama

Touch of frost, a veil so thin
Colder day and longer night
Older person with their kin
Making sure to hold them tight.
Whilst huddled round the firelight

Numbing of all appendages
Making it hard to communicate
And the peaceful nights the town envisages
As it lacks the light for those to dedicate
All that the council disparages

As those with lung ailments struggle to breathe
And children play in the ghostly snow
All of the birds begin to leave
To coasts filled with the sun's afterglow
Like the rich to their foreign chateaux

Despite all of the abrasive hail
Or the frostbitten and unforgiving dusk
The warmth of hearth and family shall prevail
The lacking enthusiasm of daylight brusque
Or the shopping hours' curtail

For winter is a time of joy
One that no creative mind can destroy.

Zachary Green (16)

A Place For Penguins

There are penguins at the door!
It's really rather strange
I think they want a holiday here
They say they need a change...

Apparently it's perfect
The cold is so refreshing.
It's an ideal town for us to stay
The temperature's a blessing!

The place where we all used to go
It's far too warm right now
(The South Pole if you didn't know)
We always wiped our brows...

If you humans weren't aware
It's all because of you
Polluting this whole planet now
All we say is true!

Global warming's causing this
Your silly engines, cars
Your factories and machinery
And all your stupid wars

Oh do let us remain here!
It's perfect in all ways
No more hot but freezing cold
It'd be cool for us to stay!

Soon the summer's coming
Temperatures to revive
We penguins have no place to go
Please help our world survive!

Indya Lilly Burke (11)

Back For Christmas

The sharp aroma of roasted chestnuts
Lingers in the dimly lit sitting room, waiting
On the roar of engines. Nothing occurs.
Nothing had arisen since the June of '09, but
Still they wait with hope in their naive eyes.
Maybe this Christmas, maybe this year
He will return from his trip, with cheery
Smiles and festive spirit.

The wax candle diminishes,
Hands clasped for warmth around cups of cocoa.
Scarves, hats and woolly jumpers.
Frosted panes and heart-felt pain,
Waiting. Still no sign. Heavy sighs.
Disappointed faces, pouting lips.

But, then.
A tap on the door jolts
Them from their grief.
Tentatively the door is opened and
In steps a middle-aged man with
A bag over his shoulder teeming
With gifts of every size and shape.

Shrill laughter breaks the silence
'You came, you came!'
'My dear sons, I'm back and here to stay.'

Molly Emery (15)

A Not-So-Jolly Season

Winter is the time of year,
When we should all be filled with cheer,
But when it's cold wet and foggy,
It's hard to stay jolly.
Even when your tree is up,
Tinsel, baubles and hot chocolate in a cup.
All you want is for school to end,
So you can play with your friends.
School seems to last forever
Even though you're much cleverer

Christmas Eve is finally here
Now we have one more reason to cheer!
Staying awake all night
Yet all you want to do is wrap up tight
Waiting for morning to come
So you can open your presents with your chum!
You get what you want plus tons more
It is so great you even drop your jaw.

Finally it's Boxing Day
The time you all say
Merry Christmas everyone!
It's time to have fun
Family presents and joy

You will get your favourite toy
Then you will play with your cousins
And eat lots of cookies, there will be dozens!

Lucy Matthews (14)

Dear Winter

You come only once a year,
Bringing songs and cheer.
Squirrels once full of mischief and fun,
Their hibernation had begun.

As your gift fell through the sky,
Us children laugh without knowing why.
Your snowflakes bring lots of joy,
But to some people it just annoys.

The coldness stiffens up their fingers.
Sitting in bed with no singers.
Their hearts frozen solid as they miss
The magic of the winter kiss.

Use your gifts to make them believe.
That this is not the same as they once received.
Your sparkling howls turn houses into cakes.
Snowmen dance in snowflakes.

Winter is the time to be spent with family.
Snuggle up together happily.
But some still cannot see,
The way it's meant to be.

You play only once a year,
Bringing lots of songs and cheer.
Share your magic with everyone,
Christmas time has begun.

Xue Lin (11)

Winter

When I woke up, it was snowing
And I saw a dark tree glowing
Pink, red, blue, green light bulbs were shining in the inky night sky.
It was cold and almost winter
It was like being in Siberia
In the coldness and darkness of the endless snow
It was so dark, like being at the peak of the world
It was time to build a snowman
But it was too dark to mould
Every morning I peeked out of the window
And wondered how cold it would be at Hanford that day.
I tried to make a snowball
But it was like a scoop of ice cream
It was as if I was holding a freezing planet
It was cold and round as if it was a ball
But when I got back from school
I found only a ball of cotton blue,
Which reminded of a planet
I almost knew

Anna Chudzik (12)

Wonders Of Winter

Our favourite time of the year is nearly here,
The time we go out to play,
And forget about our fears.
Snow boots, scarves and slippery ice,
'Are you coming out to play?'
I didn't have to think twice!

What do I enjoy most about winter?
I can tell you, it's not letting Dad get out that fresh, new splinter,
Possibly taking Mum around the shops, trying to drop hints at her.
Maybe it's the hot chocolate I always leave half drunk,
Or rocking around the Christmas tree like the next, new punk.

I enjoy searching through the drawer trying to find a glove with no hole,
Making the chocolate Christmas cake, licking clean the bowl.
Perhaps seeing the family come together - as a whole.
Seeing the snowmen lined in rows,
Trying to forget about my wet, frozen, soggy toes.

Holly Wolstenholme (15)

The Winter Sun

Scream, and it bites.
Run, and it fights.
Bitter, it withers,
'Against me it shivers,'
Says the Cold Winter Sun.

Stand, and it purrs.
Listen, it hurts.
Stalked in iced grass,
'Shielded by red glass,'
Says the Cold Winter Sun.

Win, and it keels.
Lose, and it kills.
Leaving you raving,
'A blow most unscathing,'
Mocks the Cold Winter Sun.

Give, and it takes,
take, and it breaks.
Watch yourself shatter,
'Broken and scattered,'
Claims the Cold Winter Sun.

Sit, and it listens.
Stare, and it glistens.
Lit by a dark light,
Heat cold and sun bright.
'Air frost and blood rights;
Words harsh in jealous spite,'
Says the Cold Winter Sun,
In the Cold Winter Night,

To a Cold Winter Man
bathed in frostbitten light.

Azriel Bowles (15)

Winter Is Here

Winter is coming, bringing Christmas along,
Everyone is cheerful playing in the cold snow.
Glittery icicles hanging gracefully like bats,
Trees stood bare in a group waiting patiently.
Snowballs coming face to face with me,
Covering my face with whiteness.
A white blanket of snow covering the streets.
Freezing cold air breathing upon me,
Giving me that feeling that Christmas has finally reached us.
Santa in the beautiful night sky waving 'Merry Christmas' to everyone.
Christmas trees being decorated in warm, lovely homes,
By children who are all excited.
Presents stacked happily under the Christmas tree.
Children having a fun time decorating biscuits for Santa.

I love Christmas, don't you?

Maliha Hayyat (10)

Manchester Markets

Shades of red and green paint the scenes,
The twinkle of toffee-nosed stars in a sycophantic night,
The vivacity on Manchester streets, markets jam packed.

A lifetime worth of cocoa cups I treasure in my kitchen cupboard;
I travel today to adopt a new.
An opaque innocence of cream which stains my lips.
The curl of a body cocooned within layers of wool.

Cheery smiles we share as a warm flame licks our skin.
The beautiful sins we create below le mistletoe.
Hearts strum faster, humming the tunes of Christmas carols.
Until dawn, our laughter beats hard on the pavement.

Though I wish for snow.
A glance at a review mirror; you're half lost.
I'd drive home and put you on the shelf aside the rest.
You knew all along,
You were the part of winter I liked the best.

Iqra Bibi (17)

Trees Without Leaves

The trees seem to shiver,
As their leaves have left their side,
Left bare to stand alone,
I really must confide,
I feel bad for these gnarls,
These age-old spiral limbs,
But it's nothing to compare,
To the excitement within,

My coat has been dug out again,
Frostbite begins its awful pain,
The gritty salt lies on the lane,
Winter has begun its reign,
Jumpers are layered on my back,
I can get out my stocking sack,
The shops have stocked the bauble stack,
Winter is here.

The trees seem rather happy,
Even though they don't hold leaves,
Left bare to stand there strong,
I really do believe,

I feel grateful for these gnarls,
These age-old spiral limbs,
And that's all I can compare,
To the happiness within.

Ruby Cline (13)

Winter Wonder

It's that time of year,
The rain will fall
The wind will rage
Yet it won't matter as we snuggle by the fireplace.

A hot chocolate ready
Hats and scarves adorning our bodies
The days get shorter
As little children snuggle their teddies.

Our cheeks are red
our clothes get thicker
it's official now
summer is dead.
Christmas is around the corner
yet bonfire night comes first
or maybe Halloween
The holiday of horror.

The children jump in puddles
Short sleeves are exchanged for woolly jumpers
the warmth changes to the cold
everyone begins to huddle.

You see winter is a time for wonder
For TV by the fire
Time to dig out that old Christmas tree
Maybe we'll even see some snow this year.

Megan Sutcliffe (18)

Enjoy The Day Boy

Enjoy the day boy
This night I snuggle under my bed
To wake up with a rather sleepy head
But what I see outside
Are floors of snowflakes' blanket
As I take a step in the snowy land
As the scene attracts my stone heart as if it was a magnet
To something mysterious
So, move closer because you are curious
About the golden land of grand.

This is the winter land of happiness and joy
So just enjoy the rest of the day boy.

Kindness is spread like any other day
As you will find your dream someday
Because this is the day to pay your respect
To the people who regret
Having such pain
Of neglect.

So, show your respect for the day
Because, boy it is a special day
Of happiness and joy
So just enjoy the day young boy.

Satiya Bekelcha Yaya (15)

Midwinter

Night comes early, the moon fast
Animals curl and wrap up warm,
The smell of punch and spiced orange
dances wildly through your nostrils

Warm toes curl up in wellington boots
Noses are cold and cheeks are red
A sigh of relief we're almost there

There's an element of tradition
chanting song and dark skies
A bright fire looms in the centre.

A smile of recognition, the raising
of a mug and grinning at a dancing child.
The trees hang bare spindly branches
reaching out, forking off like crossroads

A girl sits in the grass
wild ginger hair spreads like fire about her face
eyes sparkling looking into the flames
a gentle stroke of mud across her face
as she brushes her hands across the earth.

Deia Russell-Smith (17)

Snow

Falling,
Freezing,
Hopeful,
Appealing.
A flimsy fairyland
Smothering
Harsh reality.

Lying,
Misleading,
Covering footprints,
Enchanting.
Alluring,
But hides the
Hideous truth underneath.

Scintillating,
Glimmering,
Luminous,
Shimmering.
Clean and pristine,
Yet so
Tainted and flawed.

The first snowflake:
The seed of doubt.
The little white lie:
Enough to make a tree sprout.
The leaves fall down:
Relentless.
One after the other - a collection.
But the tree is soon bare; it has no protection
Because truth lives
In the midst of deception.

Mawadda Edbagi (12)

Hope

Sparkling snowflakes,
drift,
swift,
fall,
twirl.

A blanket of sugar,
dusting the roof,
a young girl,
alone.

Inside the window,
a glass of cheer,
laughter and happiness,
a single tear.

The girl outside,
face to the window,
a glimmer of hope,
she is believing.

A wreath on the door,
covered in bells,
ringing and swinging,
as the family stares.

After eternity,
the door opens wide,
a glittering smile,
lights up the sky.

Arms open fully,
the women will share,
as the young girl will enter,
and love will prevail.

Hannah Duckworth (12)

When It's Winter

When snow sprinkles down
Like icing sugar on cupcakes.
When the majestic sun scatters
Its golds and bronzes over frozen lakes.
When the moonlit sky
Glimmers at night.

When mischievous children
Play snowball fights.
When like hooting owls
The wind blows.
When frost is nipping
At your nose.

When Christmas cards
Are given out.
When New Year's Eve
Is a total blowout!

When it's time
You caught a cold.
When your dad
Has just shaved you bald!

When you snuggle up in bed
Thinking, 'What a day!'
But too many sweets
Cause teeth to decay!

Amin Edbagi (11)

I Love Christmas!

I love Christmas because of the joy
The snow that sparkles on Christmas morning
The snowman that has a carrot for a nose,
The wreath that goes on the door

I love Christmas because of the presents underneath the tree
The tree that lights up like stars in the midnight sky
How I love the stocking hanging over the fireplace

I love Christmas because of the carols
The carols that are catchy and fun,
The ones that makes you forget all of the things that you have done.
The most important thing about Christmas is...

Family
The people you eat Christmas dinner with
The people you spend your whole life with
But that special moment means the most.

And that's all I love about Christmas.

Laurna Yeboah

The Little Matchstick Girl

Out there... somewhere - very far
They tell me there is no cold!
Winter, started with my fears
And ended by my tears.

Out there... somewhere - very far
A little jolly soul plays with the snow
And here I am freezing my heart
Waiting for it to wither... So I can feel pain, no more.

Out there... somewhere - very far
A family is born!
But here I am with a heart completely torn.

Out there... somewhere - very far
There are remnants of those I love
But, I can see them no more
For I have lost them all...

Inside here... somewhere - very near
A glimmer appears!
Winter, the candle of hope and faith,
That will illuminate my dark days
Just like the sun that will come out when the dawn is nigh.

Mawada Ben Taher (15)

Winter

The sky is dark and the ground is white,
The world is peaceful on this wintry night,
Not a sound was heard,
Snow passing by made me blurred,
Winter is once again back,
Now the evenings will be fully pitch-black.

Christmas has finally arrived,
Now everyone's excitement has returned,
Loads of wishes and presents shall be received,
Let Christmas proceed,
Let the harsh breeze dance through the air,
While the celebrations begin.

Winter has now ended,
Our happiness is fading away,
No gifts until next year,
A long way to bear,
This year was fun,
But I cannot wait for *next year!*

Claudia Anton (12)

Christmas Time Is Here

Christmas time is here
Glass baubles hung from the fir tree as little lights flashed all around,
a thick streak soared across the sky through the window,
sleigh bells ringing and reindeer whinnying,
the fire crackling and spitting and parcel wrapping strewn across the floor,
a mouth-watering aroma of turkey and sprouts
drifted up everyone's nostrils
as they banged their knives and forks against the table,
snow spread on the inside of the snow globe
covering the Virgin Mary and baby Jesus,
scenes of joy and light could be seen inside people's warm homes,
smiles and grins lit up people's faces whilst looks of surprise on others.

Megan Elizabeth Waite (10)

Snow Season

Another autumn has gone by,
But that's typical for time to fly,
As children come outside to play,
Animals sleep throughout the day,
But there is a place,
An enchanted place,
Where crystals of ice fall with grace,
Trees of ice,
Flowers of snow,
White ripples in streams,
A sky of never-ending dreams,
A land of white,
A sky of blue,
A sparkled halation,
This much is true,
Trees stand bare,
Icy winds sing,
Vines that snare,
Winter bells ring,
Soon the sky will be filled with colour,
Fireworks here, there,
Boom, crash everywhere,
People will stand,
They look amazed,

Suddenly from no where,
A Christmas band,
Winter is a wonderful time,
But what I love,
A winter wonderland.

Jakir Ali (15)

Festive Frivolities

The boiler whirs and rattles away,
As I drink my hot chocolate with glee,
Jingle bells ring on an outdoor sleigh,
As I look at the gleaming Christmas tree,

Elves craft toys for boys and girls,
Those children who still believe,
Reindeer are fed for the journey ahead,
The snowy ride of Christmas Eve,

Santa shakes his belly in his jolly red suit,
Prepared and ready for his annual adventure,
The sleigh and reindeer take to the sky,
As the moon silhouettes an antlered creature,

Winter is joy,
So full of snow,
Winter is uplifting,
Leaving my heart aglow.

Niamh Caroline Chalmers (11)

A Winter's Night

I lay on my back staring at the night sky,
shielded by snow below the shimmering stars.
I waved and waved my feeble arms through the snow,
not feeling a thing, I was numb to my toes.
I strolled around the town seeing trees of no colour,
their coats had been poached by the chilly iced winter.
Still mesmerised, I stood, Jack Frost nibbled at my nose,
as I wondered and wondered where the squirrels had roamed.
At last it was time to go back inside,
to drink my hot chocolate, stretch my legs by the fire.
But don't worry, I thought about my new friends,
for I had left my snow angels to guard my snowmen.

Saman Shahzad (14)

A Winter's Dream

The cold snowy ice lays upon the lake.
The snow falls and the decorations are laid.
Shovelling snow in the late-night glow
As the snow falls slow, slow, slow.
Hot chocolate is made and marshmallows are roasting
The frosty grass blows and the morning dew begins to form.
As the morning falls and the fun begins
As we build our snowmen with their wings,
The hats are on, the scarves are tight
As we have our snowball fight
As the night draws in the campfire is lit
We sing and bite on our honey sticks,
Put your PJs on because I'm feeling dozy, and I want to get cosy
As the beautiful dark night comes to an end.

Lily Bennett (10)

The Beautiful Winter Sight

The fragile snow fell to the ground,
It piled up without making a sound,
The winter sun was slowly rising,
The sight was truly tranquilising,
The children woke up and looked outside,
When they saw the pure white snow their eyes went wide.

They were soon out playing in the snow,
Getting snowballs ready to throw,
The little snowflakes continue to fall,
But then they heard their mother call,
'Time to come in you have had your fun,'
But then she threw a snowball and shouted, 'I won!'

It was now dark so you could tell it was night,
And now you had to wait till morning to see the beautiful winter sight.

Maggie Old-Gooch (13)

Is It Winter Yet?

The snow is beginning to fall
Mum's buying hats, scarves and gloves
My brothers are complaining that it's too cold
Is it winter yet?

The trees are growing bare
And they're growing dull too
The leaves are falling everywhere
Is it winter yet?

Snowmen are appearing in all the gardens
Children are taking their sleighs up hills
Hot chocolate is being served in the evenings
Is it winter yet?

Icicles hang from the windowpane
My breath hangs in the air
Frost covers the car's windscreen
It's winter now!

Thalia Warren (10)

A Day In The Winter Wonderland

Snow is fun,
Snow is cold.
Fun when you're with that certain one,
You never know what winter holds.

When you go around that bend,
In the crunching snow.
I see my small red friend,
Mr Robin who always knows.

My time is over in the snow,
My dinner's ready, I need to go.
Got my favourite meal, chicken on the bone,
I go to my room and spend some time on my own.

I'm tired out, I'm going to sleep,
Tonight my dream is going to be deep.
Tomorrow will be another day,
And I can go out and play.

Danny Joseph Byrne (11)

Christmas Is Coming!

Make sure you wrap your presents,
and write your Christmas cards.
Make sure you stay asleep,
in waiting for Santa's bodyguards.
Bake the mince pies, pour the milk,
and be sure to leave a carrot.
As the reindeer will be hungry,
from flying the magic chariot.
Roast marshmallows on the fire,
and dip the chestnuts in salt.
Remember the steps in making s'mores,
make sure you do not fault.
Wake up on Christmas morning,
and eat the last piece of advent.
Open your presents, eat lots of food,
and I'll see you on the next event!

Imogen Barr (13)

Chocolate In Snow

Puff? Puff? Puff?
Snots in coughs,
Couple of steps
on refrigerated paths.
Footsteps squelching, digging heavily into marshmallow fluff.
Holding a mug with fingers in frostbite? Tough?
Containing hot chocolate filled up halfway down the mug.
So is that enough?
Tiptoeing, hesitating, camouflaging... oops
A little mischief took place due to the sabotage of the cup.
A thick layer of chocolate, splashed across the snow.
Her tiny grin stood out showing a laughter of her tiny naughtiness.
Neighbours called out, 'Merry Christmas!'
A nearby footstep echoed *puff, puff, puff...*

Kewen Wang (13)

I Love Christmas

I love the way snow falls to the crisp white ground,
and the way it flies care-free, without a sound,
the way children happily bounce around.

I love the way dramatic dancers glide through the night,
and how the evil spirits stay hidden, out of sight,
the way screaming candles burn with such a light.

I love the way heavenly singers sing songs of glee,
and how the thoughtful gifts lay waiting, under the tree,
the way spiritful people realise they are free.

I love Christmas, I never want to flee,
but most of all I love the people that spend it with me.

Tanica Cherelle Karen Anderson (13)

Winter Paradise

I look out of the window,
the one down by the hall,
I see blankets of white creamy snow
and as the moon and stars get ready for nightfall.

Silhouettes in the distance throwing balls of vaporised frozen ice,
become less as they go into the entrance of winter paradise.

The breeze of fresh, cool air chants a melody,
as the trees dance along endlessly.

Looking back to the spot,
I see icicles of diamonds that start to heavenly drop.

The place I know, the one by the gate
that treasures not only snow but a wonderful winter paradise.

Nia Joseph (11)

Wintertime

In the winter the snow falls down,
I love to run and have snowball fights,
I make my snowman a little crown,
Which by then he is jolly and bright,
The best part of winter is when we all eat,
My family and me have a big dinner,
This is when we all like to meet,
Then we play a game and I am the winner,
When we are finished, we have our dessert,
After dessert we are full,
While Mummy and Daddy start to flirt,
Everybody feels as fat as a bull,
Now it's time to rest my head,
In my soft and quite warm bed.

Kaytie Alexander-Smith (13)

The Eye Of The Beholder

Oh, how times can change and repeat without afterthought of repentance or grief,
With no further objections than to freeze autumn's first fallen leaf
Or dress trees' desolate branches with new life and vibrancy.
As we watch autumn drift into a darkened daybreak and white horizons,
With wide eyes staring on in disbelief
As they scurry through a wasteland of brilliant white
That glistens like a fresh page in the chilling winter sun,
We can finally experience the beauty Mother Nature has birthed,
In the eye of the beholder.

Toni Alice Crompton (13)

Christmas Eve

C hristmas is a time for joy,
H elpers come and deliver some toys.
R eally happy I bet you are,
I n the sky a shining star.
S itting on the table the candles are lit,
T he baby is wearing its Christmas knits.
M ight even chew on some beef jerky,
A t the table eating delicious turkey,
S now covering the lakes which are murky.

E ven now the Christmas spirit is spread,
V ery nearly time for bed.
E xcited for Christmas, the day ahead.

Maariyah Mumtahanah Syed

Winter Wonderland

The icy wind blows and makes the leafless trees swing,
it dances around, it whispers, it sings
The white frosted snow, each one so unique,
it falls for miles until, at last, it lands right on my cheek
The city is covered with a layer of snow,
purification from all the months of pollution from the road show
A winter wonderland is what awaits my eyes
as the last breeze of autumn slowly subsides
A world where fairies could one day reign
in a white world where cities are rid of their pain
A new, undiscovered, area of land,
that is my Winter Wonderland.

Virtudes Miralles (14)

He Looks At Me

I breathe out,
I breathe in.
Inside my nose
The cold air does sting.
The sudden chill
Is exhilarating.

He looks at me,
I look at him.
I turn away
And shyly grin.
I wait, for I
Know what is coming.

I feel snowflakes on my nose
And hear shuffling.
I feel impact on my back,
My coat is thin
And water from snow seeps through
Cooling my skin.

I turn around,
Giggling,
Scoop up a handful
Of snow, and lob it at him.

Rosa-May Bown (14)

You And Me

A chill sets into the cool winter's air
A cold lover's kiss, a gentle caress
We huddle by the fireplace, you and me
As the sun begins to set
The night begins to creep

An excited gasp escapes your lips
Tiny fist clutching fish and chips
We dance around in circles, hand in hand
6-year-old heart is brimming with joy
Walking in a winter wonderland

Sugar plums and snowflakes, stockings, stars
Twinkle in your eye, another childish laugh
Santa's sleigh? Perhaps not quite
But I will rock you in my arms
Until the morning light.

Grace Gbadamosi (14)

Excitement

The Christmas tree is glowing,
The stockings are on the wall,
The moonlight glows above the trees,
And the snow begins to fall.

My nose is red like Rudolph,
Who will be visiting very soon,
And Santa and his other reindeer,
Will be shadows against the moon.

The fire glows and crackles,
There is warmness in the air,
We all sing and dance to music,
Because at this time we don't care!

No one can doubt that feeling,
At Christmas it's always there,
It twinkles more than the stars glow,
It is excitement, pure as air!

Freya Cerys Ashworth (12)

The Magical Aftermath Of Snow

Opening curtains,
The magical aftermath
Of snow just appears.

The bare tree branches,
Who spooked us all of autumn,
Are covered in snow.

Countdown to Christmas,
To the jolliest event,
Finally begun.

Now we must reach deep
Into a wardrobe for hats,
Scarves and mitten gloves.

This pure wonderland,
Is filled with children's laughter,
And throwing snowballs.

Our forgotten friends,
Asymmetrical snowmen,
Await children's hugs.

Closing the curtains,
Lying under warm blankets,
Hoping snow will stay.

Nataliya Klymko (14)

The Warmth Of Winter

Trees come toppling down ready to go to homes,
As the blanket of snow acts as a large pit of foam,
All the children at home playing round the tree,
The words flow like water, as they come to me.

An amazing sight that you will know,
Is winter's first flake of snow,
Given all these beautiful wintertime things,
There's still the feast that Christmas brings.

And then there's the night that Santa comes,
When early awakenings lead to satisfied hums,
Then follows laughter, thanks and joy,
From every good girl and boy.

Lucia Cyples (10)

Having Fun Together

Families and friends come together at last,
To have a good time together it's going to be a blast,
Having dinner the same every year,
Eating it together spreading the best kind of cheer.

Having fun snowball fights,
Putting up great bright lights,
Telling funny jokes for fun,
Playing games (we hope you've won).

Having a smile on your face,
Knowing that this is your home, your place,
Building a snowman with your friend,
Wishing the day will never end.

Winter, the time to spend with family and friends.

Georgia Anne Ellis (12)

The Other Side Of Christmas

The dark astounds me.
No one really knows
What could be hiding out there.
It's a mystery that
No one can solve.
Lights, draped around trees,
Wreaths on doors and fires
Glowing in their grates.
Has no one considered that maybe
The fires are drawing in
The monsters!
Slowly but surely,
Luring them in with promises
Of milk and cookies,
Eggnog and carols by the fire.
Of children swaddled in blankets,
Unable to escape from their cocoons.
They blossom at Christmas,
Come out from their shells:
Creatures of nightmares.

Isha Lamba (15)

Ice Skating Queen

My dream can begin,
The lake is iced.
Bring out my desire within,
Thank you my Lord Christ.

Winter brings me,
Not only Christmas presents,
Or festive peace,
But my heart's content.

I rush for my skates,
I sprint for my mittens.
I arrive there to see my mates,
Supporting me and all these skating women.

I'm not mean,
I'm not vain.
But I am the Ice Skating Queen,
And winter long holds my reign.

Shannon Rose Byrne (15)

Christmas Snow

As quiet as a mouse,
Tip-toe tip-toe without a creak.
Open the door,
Guess what there is,
Presents, presents and more presents.
The presents had brightly coloured paper wrapping.

I look outside I suddenly realise,
'It's snowing it's snowing!' I whisper, to myself.
The snow is as white as a dove.

With the snow I can make angels,
With the snow we can have snowball fights.
With the snow I can make snowmen,
With the snow we can go down hills on toboggan sledges,
'Weeeee!'

Niall Smith (10)

My Christmas Time Rhyme

Do you know the news?
It's getting cold,
The big day's coming soon;
Have you heard the rhyme,
Of Christmas time?
Well here I go, listen well;
Do you hear the ringing? It's Santa's bells,
He's covered in red from head to toe,
It's almost Christmas time,
So listen to the winter rhyme,
It goes:
Do you know the news?
It's getting cold,
The big day's coming soon,
It's almost Christmas time!

Chelsie Wheat (10)

Seasons Of The Snow

I've never seen a sight so pretty
A sparkling blanket covering cities
Where rain and sun cease to exist
And snow begins to fall once more
Then small white coats glide on ice
And families finally reunite
The saddest of fellows frolic merrily in the snow
A break from the world far below
To remember other years further back
While telling tales by a radiant fire
My favourite season has finally come
It's here
Winter is here everyone.

Ruqaiyah Jarviton (12)

Winter Prayer

My windowpane is starred with frost,
The world is bitter cold tonight,
The moon is cruel, and the wind
Is like a two-edged sword to smite.

God pity all the homeless ones,
The beggars pacing to and fro.
God pity all the poor tonight
Who walk the lamp-lit streets of snow.

My room is like a bit of June,
Warm and close-curtained fold on fold,
But somewhere, like a homeless child,
My heart is crying in the cold.
Wish I could be there
Wish I could be there
Least I can do is pray for all.

Fatimah Isap (10)

A World Below

S nowflakes drift gently to the world below,
N oels to who we hold dear we bestow.
O nce I hear those sleigh bells ring,
W inter's bleakness starts to sing.
F inally close to the ones I love,
L inked together like hand in glove.
A new year's start can make dreams come true,
K indling aspirations anew.
E verlasting joy to the ones we know,
S nowflakes drift gently to the world below.

Laura Prentice (14)

Frostbite

The ague breaks out of me
everything is covered
with the rawness of a blanket
the world disappears in front of me

I've been working all day
this place belongs to me
my worn out jumper is my only hope
of keeping my fingers hidden from my only friend

she will take me away no matter what I tell her
her first name is gelidity
and her surname is frostbite
she is the one

the more you want her to go the more she comes
so don't run away because you will be gone.

Maariyaah Khan (13)

Natalie's Christmas Poem

C is for Christmas that everyone loves
H is for happiness that shines in your eyes
R is for reindeer that fly in the sky
I is for ice that is slippery and cold
S is for snow that falls outside
T is for trees that we decorate every year
M is for mince pies that Santa loves to eat
A is for angels that guide the way to the stables
S is for Santa who is the most magical of all.

Natalie May Foster (10)

Warm In Here

Hibernating in my warmest blanket and my cosiest onesie,
Drinking hot chocolate that burns my tongue
As I sit next to the warm fire while looking out at the winter snow,
Being grateful I'm not out there - freezing,
Wearing a coat and gloves and a hat,
Falling in the yellow snow,
And being hit by freezing ice balls which sounds like fun but really isn't.
So as I watch you out there - cold,
I'll be in here - warm.

Keira Parker (15)

Winter Poem

A gentle kiss against my cheek
Every single flake completely unique
A voice whispering in my ears
Although what it says is not too clear

The ground is paper, my footprints are ink
and as the sun comes up my heart sinks

Tall green trees some made of plastic
With blinking stars attached to it

I love the winter season
For many, many reasons

And I have to say as the weeks go on
I'm not looking forward to waking up to a bird song.

Tia Flanagan (14)

Alone In The World

Crystallised branches,
A fragile blanket of snow,
Frozen breath
Pursues like a shadow.

Footprints hidden,
Hidden by the ice.
Warmth forbidden,
Forbidden to be nice.

Enveloped in white,
Unable to see,
But for the golden light
That lets us be free.

Alone in the world
Capturing me,
Resisting its fate...
The evergreen tree.

Anastasia Armstrong (12)

Winter Has Arrived!

Fragile snowflakes descend from the sky,
Shops are stacked with fresh mince pies.
While the streets beam with multicoloured lights,
Houses are smothered with thick chunks of white.

Wrapped up like a present, the people hurry along,
While the radios are chiming old winter songs.
As I sip my creamy hot chocolate in delight,
Observing this beautiful nippy winter night.

Chanice Esther Barrow (16)

Christmas Day

It's Christmas day, it's Christmas day
As I walked across the snow,
I felt the winter's frigid wind blow
I still can't believe it, it's Christmas day hooray!

My presents are under the Christmas tree,
That Santa gave to me,
All my family are here with me
It's Christmas day, it's Christmas Day

The jolly day has come to an end,
But it was great fun,
Merry Christmas, everyone!

Chantel Edwards (13)

Winter

No leaves left to be seen,
Ice covering fields that used to be green,
What used to be a gentle wind is now a bitter breeze,
Numb fingers, shivering knees.

Evenings spent by the fire,
All I have is one present desire,
Icicles hang from every window,
Trees dripping with snow.

Christmas is only around the bend,
This year is coming to an end,
Presents wait under the tree,
Families filled with glee.

Eve Newman (13)

Winter

Flesh pierced by frost
Winter conquers all,
Snowflakes forever lost
While swirling at the ball

Cold limbs, scorching hearts
Spilling with melted fire,
The darkness starts
To devour with desire.

Chocolaty heaven leaves
Scalding streaks dripping
From my chin, it weaves
The icy sinews of my heart

A shadow trembles
While the moon supervises,
The silence dissembles,
The mist paralyses.

Patricia Popa (14)

Winter's Night

Everything is silent,
Daybreak is yet to rise,
I'm ready and raring for the day ahead,
As I search the starry skies.
The cosiness of home engulfs me,
The fire glistens in the dark,
The windows are dense with condensation,
A cacophony of crackling bark.
Flakes of snow glimmer,
Falling softly from up above,
Small flurries glisten in the rare stream of light,
And I watch with wonder and love.

Jodie Stone (13)

The Snowman

I am a snowman, cold and white
I stand so still through all the night.
With a carrot nose,
And head held high,
And a lump of coal to make each eye
The morning comes and the
Sun is coming out - oh my!
I think that I might as well cry,
Yesterday, I had so much fun with
The children playing all night long,
Yesterday I was so happy and round,
Now the sun is out I'm just a river on the ground!

Courtney Leigh (16)

Christmas To Me

The smell of peppermint,
The falling of snow,
Santa is coming soon,
Didn't you know?

Gifts are being passed out,
And the lights are on the tree.
Joy is all around,
Everyone is as happy as can be...

The turkey's in the oven,
The vegetables are chopped,
My family is gathered round,
The fun cannot be stopped!

Amy Stewart (14)

Listen To Winter's Song

Listen, listen
Listen to Winter's song
Winter sings quietly it doesn't want anyone to know
When it's snowing and the snowflakes are dancing around
That's how you know Winter's singing its song
As it sings, it wipes all the clouds away
We know it as wind
But it's Winter chanting away
Winter's song is the best song of all
Because it allows unity to grow.

Tehillah Honny (12)

A Winter Scene

Frozen flakes float
Down to the ground
Like autumn leaves did
One season ago

Leaving branches bare
Lined with snow
And painted with care
Like sugary icing
Dusted across the lands
The hill tops and moors
By professional hands
Littered with frost sores

Meanwhile soft white
Buttercream slopes
Fall from cold roof tiles
Whilst wool-clad locals
Shovel the snow into piles.

Atlanta Jade Revill (13)

A Winter's Dream

Slowly you drift down,
Colliding with the others,
How far will you go?

Cold yet delicate,
Each and every, I adore,
Well, until you melt.

Outside my window,
Lays the cool serenity,
A blanket above.

How long you will last?
Days, weeks, months, I'll never know,
I wish it would last.

An eternity,
Frozen forever in time,
I wish it were true.

Sinead Cheung

Wintertime

From furry coats to icy roads,
To getting presents, I have loads!
From all the snow,
To the Christmas glow,
I love Santa!
It's no banter!
Wintertime is simply awesome,
Mum, pull me closer.
Make a smiling snowman;
Eat a gingerbread man.
Look, I have a frozen finger,
Because I love winter!

Maria Manta (11)

Festival Of Colours

Gleaming bright eyes dance in the shadows of the burning embers
Flickering flames hug souls tightly
Ash flutters around its mother
Sweet treats melt in the flames of hope and trust
Bang!
A kaleidoscope of colours engulfs the once bland landscape
Crash!
The joyful spells descend as gasping voices whisper on the wind
Silence...

Georgie von Grundherr (14)

Cold Winter

Wonderful winter,
in December,
never a bad season,
keeping warm,
sometimes when it's down,
with your family,
playing outside,
while the snow arrives,
just above your head,
making snowmen too,
season changing,
every year,
can't wait for spring again...

Zeinab Wnis (10)

Winter Times...

At the times of winter snow,
Flakes might fall for all you know.
Snow will plummet down and fall,
As it brings the joy for all.
All the creatures hibernate,
While they greatly grew and ate.
As the children laughed and played,
Every tree just swiftly swayed.
At the end of winter season,
They were sad for every reason.

Priyan Yaddehige

My Snowball Called Holly

I made a snowball called Holly
She was really jolly
Mum told me to come inside
I didn't want to leave her side
So I took her inside
She escaped when I entered the front door
Leaving a wee stain in my sight
I was full of fright
I think she has gone for the night.

Todah Honny

The Light Of Winter

One night a star shone in the sky,
people gazed and pointed,
who knew a gem could be so high.
The rockets launched but it was just out of reach,
but then they realised it was there for each
child and adult to see and say,
'What a beautiful star I saw today.'

Maizy Day (10)

An Animal's Winter

Freezing penguins cuddle up tight,
As icy cold winds pass their soft black heads.
Cosy and chubby hedgehogs hibernate in the soft, cold leaves.
Birds fly south, as it starts to get colder.
Squirrels gather nuts ready for when the trees go bare.

Keira Harvey (10)

The Chill Of The Gale

The chill of the gale tickles the spine
The pitch winter's night
Warmed only by mulled wine
The glow of the fire
Enticing with heat
Devours the logs from beneath its feet
Tiny white specks drift down towards Earth
Dancing in wind
Celebrating the birth.

Shannon Clack (17)

Winter Is...

Winter is white,
Winter is cold,
Winter is wet,
Winter is bold.

Winter is Christmas,
Winter is a feeling,
Winter is playing,
Winter is December.

Winter is all those things
and many more, but the best
thing of winter is snow and no more.

Kira Mullen (10)

Christmas Is Here Soon

Christmas is here soon
So stay up till noon
Opening your Christmas presents
Throwing snowballs at your friends
It never ends
Turkey and Brussels sprouts
Holly and stockings
Santa is coming to town
So don't be down
'Cause Christmas is here.

Usman Siddiqui (10)

The Snowflake

Children dance and play in the snow,
Waiting for Father Christmas to say hello.

Whilst the children sleep,
The snowflakes leap
and dance and play in the snow.

Tayla Alison Schofield (13)

Snowflakes

Snowflakes falling,
Winter is here,
People are playing,
Catch them or they'll disappear,

Hurry up before they melt,
Quickly look then they're gone,
Be sure not to dwell.

Hafsa Hussain (13)

Wintertime Rhyme

The smells of the cinnamon and apple candles,
of the fresh, crisp, pine trees.
The sounds of jingle bells and joy,
and the robin's song, filled with glee.
The warmth of the fireplace, the burning logs,
of the hot chocolate in your mug.
The bleakness of the frosty trees,
when you are home, all warm and snug.
The craving for gingerbread, truffles, mince pies,
fruit cake and candy canes.
The view from the icy windows,
with snow on the window panes.
The stockings filled right to the top,
with presents peeking out.
The children warm in scarves and hats,
desperate to go out and about.
The Christmas crackers on the table,
that everyone desires to pull.
The hats we wear at Christmas dinner,
the dinner we eat till we're full.
The time you spend with family,
the precious memories made.

The pretty wrapped up presents we love,
to guess, unwrap, and trade.
The beautiful baubles, the tinsel and lights,
embroidering the tree.
These are the things that make my Christmas,
just so special to me.

Jessica Jane Ross (14)
Bathgate Academy, Bathgate

A Sprinkle Of Winter

The white falls out of the sky,
Down to the ground where it lies,
The sun begins to cry,
As the moon opens his eyes.

The stars begin to twinkle,
As the bells rhythmically jingle,
All the ice glistens,
As the children eagerly listen.

The snow began to shimmer,
All the icicles started to glimmer,
The sleigh bells started to ring,
As the carollers decided to sing.

Elizabeth Snedden (14)
Bathgate Academy, Bathgate

The Night Sky

Shimmering snow
As cold as iced water
Glimmers in the day
From bright morning rise.

Cold clouds
As soft as a cotton ball
Cover up
The night sky.

Misty moon
Hiding behind shadows
Is a howling wolf
Touches the winter snow.

Swirling storms
Cover a wooden lodge
Creates a topping of icing
On gingerbread houses.

Silent snow drops
Tickle your nose
Twinkling stars way up high
Lighten up the night sky.

Laura Williams (11)
Cranbrook Education Campus, Exeter

A Winter's Night

White clouds of candyfloss
Next to the night sky
Dark, cold winter's night.
Naughty shadows glide across the snow
Tall trees collect
Their night-time blanket.
Mountains smothered
In a layer of cream
Houses covered in thick coats
The black, brittle soil
Creeps through white ice.

Millie Downham-Elphick (11)
Cranbrook Education Campus, Exeter

When Santa Is On His Way!

Christmas lights are flashing,
Children are laughing,
Baubles of all colours everywhere,
People dashing here and there,
When Santa's on his way!

The carol choir is singing,
People from all over listening,
Sitting warm by the fire,
With a hot chocolate to keep me warm,
When Santa's on his way!

The Christmas stalls are open,
Presents are being sold,
The Christmas tree is being decorated,
While the presents sit under the tree,
When Santa's on his way!

Finally it's Christmas Eve,
The snow is falling softly,
Children sleeping quietly,
Rudolph dancing through the air,
The mince pie is left out but not for long,
Santa's been and gone.
When Santa's on his way!

Sophie Berry (11)
Harrogate Ladies' College, Harrogate

Christmas Day!

'Jingle bells, jingle bells,
Jingle all the way.
Oh what fun it is to ride,
In a one horse open sleigh.'

Children's voices echo the streets,
As they sweetly sing Christmas carols.
The snow is falling all around them,
As they prepare for Christmas Day!

The streets are flooding with Christmas spirit,
Everyone is full of happiness and joy.
Nothing can compare to Christmas Day,
It is the best time of the year!

Stockings by the fireplace,
Baubles on the tree.
Bright lights everywhere,
On Christmas Eve.

'Jingle bells, jingle bells,
Jingle all the way.
Oh what fun it is to ride,
In a one horse open sleigh,
Hey!'

Sophie McHugh (11)
Harrogate Ladies' College, Harrogate

A Winter Wonderland

'We wish you a merry Christmas,
we wish you a merry Christmas,
and a happy new year.'

The sweet sound of
children singing was in the air,
'The snow is falling all around us,
children playing, having fun.'

The streets were full
with joyful people.
Everywhere you go all
you see is children with snow.

No other season can compete
with winter.
Stockings hung with care,
ornaments on the tree.

The joy on Christmas morning
getting to open your presents.

'Good tidings we bring
to you and your king,
we wish you a merry Christmas
and a happy new year.'

Aimee Lauren Thomas (11)
Harrogate Ladies' College, Harrogate

Christmas Time Is Here

When lights are flashing
Rudolph is dashing
When snowflakes are falling
Christmas time is here.

Everyone is gathered together
When people have been loved forever
People are having fun
That means Christmas time is here.

Baubles are glowing
When it's time to go to bed, the fire needs blowing
Put the stockings up
And then Christmas time is here.

When the chapel choir is singing
And everyone is listening
Your heart is warmed
And Christmas time is here.

When people have no home
And they feel like they are alone
Go and raise their spirit
And then their Christmas time is here.

Ella Teale (11)
Harrogate Ladies' College, Harrogate

Christmas Cheer

Christmas is a time for true happiness and cheer,
'Christmas Day,' the child explains,
'The best day of the year!'

The angel on the tree,
Looks around and sees,
Mince pies and glistening eyes,
Under the tree a big surprise.

All those years ago, Christ was born,
And Herod's long reign was torn.
With donkeys and sheep,
Mary and Joseph's lives were sweet.

Just imagine, the love throughout,
And listen to the children shout:
'Look, the holly on the mantelpiece,'
This Christmas will never cease.

Emily-Anne Jones (12)
Harrogate Ladies' College, Harrogate

Snow Is Falling

Snow is falling in light flakes,
while people have supper with lots of cakes,
with snow everywhere,
you can't have a single foe.
Smiles on every face,
every house tile covered in snow.
Even though it's very cold, there isn't a grumble,
for snowflakes drift down to the ground.
That all anyone can mumble is behold,
Christmas is here!
Snow is falling,
it's time for Santa so you better watch out.
Snow is falling,
everything will be white,
no doubt!

Niamh Currie (12)
Harrogate Ladies' College, Harrogate

Winter Is Coming

Winter is coming!
As the biting snow trickles around,
The wind is making a howling sound,
With surprises coming every dawn,
And lights and fire to keep you warm.

Winter is coming!
It has presents, trees and treats galore,
You never know what will come through the door,
When suddenly you hear a noise,
Shiver, trickle and much more fear,
When all of a sudden you realise something is near.

Winter is coming!

Cerys Young (11)
Harrogate Ladies' College, Harrogate

Christmas Spirit

'On the first day
of Christmas, my
true love sent to me,'
the sound of the
carol singers on a
frosty night.
Everywhere you go
you couldn't escape
the jolly sound of
the carols.

Snow was falling
heavily,
streets crowded with
bustling Christmas
cheer.
Smoke wafting out
of chimneys,
from warm, open
fires.

Hannah Grant (11)
Harrogate Ladies' College, Harrogate

The Christmas Poem

People ice skating, having fun,
Trees are glistening in the sun.
Lights are shining,
Santa is timing.
The reindeer are ready to pull the sleigh,
They have been ready since May.

Children are writing,
Santa is almost arriving.
The snow is white,
It looks like it will be frosty tonight.
London is gleaming,
The Christmas pudding is steaming.

Sofia Jarman (11)
Harrogate Ladies' College, Harrogate

A White Christmas

Glistening snow covers the town
Beautiful snowflakes are coming down
As Christmas begins to look white
Santa is coming tonight
Outside the town glistens with snow
It makes the whole town glow
As I sit with hot chocolate by the fire
I dream of Santa coming with presents I desire
And when I drift to sleep that night
I see his sleigh in the sky shining bright.

Summer Elbortoukaly (11)
Harrogate Ladies' College, Harrogate

Night In The Snow

The night is a sea,
Snow is as white as sugar,
It is cold as ice.

I am a season,
The coldest of all seasons
What season am I?

I am the winter,
The favourite of all kids,
I'm white as a wall.

There's no one like me,
What do you think about it?
I have many gifts.

In the night he comes,
Singing: 'Ho, ho, ho' to kids,
Santa Claus he is.

The New Year is near,
What are you waiting in it?
Some tests? Good girlfriends?

Better help cooking,
All the family is coming,
Better help with that!

They all went long ago,
Oh no! One more year for it!
Better start counting!

Oh, winter finished!
But next year will be another,
I'm waiting for it!

Victoria Castro (12)
Holy Mary Catholic School, Madrid

Suspicious Of Christmas

I've always been very suspicious of Christmas
How it's been taken over by business.
I think it's wrong to take a time of great joy and song
And twist it into a game of marketing ping-pong;
It's just completely wrong.

But let's not be so cynical,
Because Christmas is the pinnacle.
It's about time with family and friends,
Pulling the cracker from both ends
And sitting down to a Christmas dinner that transcends.

I just love Christmas...
But it starts in October, or is it September?
I just can't remember,
It's completely relentless.
But we all know Christmas really starts when we're told to buy, buy, buy,
By people like John Lewis and M&S.
They all hit the bullseye when Christmas is nigh.
How can they justify using a soppy ad, to nullify
The public into spending money on their oversupply
Of toys and games to satisfy the outcry of the self-indulgent greed.
But what about those we don't feed?

The ones who don't pull the cracker from both ends.
The ones who don't sit down to a Christmas dinner that transcends...

What about them?

It's an ugly truth people avoid and deny,
But can't because of the occasional charity ad on Sky.
These are the people the media pass by,
The ones who hear a war cry instead of an outcry.
The ones who flee their homes while their friends die at the hands of ISIS
While the ice is being put in your drink.

So this Christmas, let's not forget this.

Max Harrison (12)
Lewes Old Grammar School, Lewes

Snow

The snow is as fluffy as a bunny.
It is ice-cold and makes you want a Slush Puppy.
Snowball fights are fun
but in the end you always get done.
The snow nips my toes, the frost nips my nose.
When you get inside in front of the fire,
your toes warm up and you can put the fire higher.
I look outside, I know he is here;
he's painted my windows with paint that's clear.
I love the Christmas theme, the snow feels just like cream.
Soft and nice just like rice.

Billy Adams (13)
Royds School, Leeds

Snow Day

Mr Frost painted my dad's car last night,
The snow is as soft as a bird's feather,
The sky is clear and dead,
No birds, no animals, no nothing,
The bright winter sun shines as bright as a diamond,
Also the sea as dark as a man's beard,
The ocean's waters are cold,
And filled with waves and others.
It is silent apart from one noise,
The screaming scary children running round,
Like the headless chickens of the forgotten summer.

Ben Russell (12)
Royds School, Leeds

Winter

Winter is the best
Don't go out in your vest
It is always cold
So put on a hat if you're bald
Although it's cold and fun
You never see the sun
The snow nips my toes
And the cold hits my nose
When you're covered in snow
You'll be absolutely freezing
So don't lie down
Or you'll be sneezing.

Alfie Mortimer (13)
Royds School, Leeds

The Snow

The snow.
It was like a blanket of ice and slush on the ground
and it was everywhere.
The snow desolately glided down to the soft, slippery grass.
The snow, as white as a fluffy cloud hovering in the sky
The snow, as cold as the North Pole, trickled down the roof to the concrete ground
The snow...
The snow...

Zach Jones (12)
Royds School, Leeds

Snow Day

The weather glared at me,
It started to snow,
The sheet of snow went past,
It was beautiful and really fast,
The snow filled my street,
The frosty flowers went away,
God painted my windows last night,
He was nice and very polite,
The snow went faster than a plane,
Then my area was boring, old and plain.

Callum Eric James Ibbotson (12)
Royds School, Leeds

Cold

I was fireside when he arrived with his frosty, fleecy blanket that covered my garden,
It looked so soft but so slippery,
The fire was crisp,
I went outside and the icy air kissed me on the cheek,
The sun was climbing now but that just made me colder
And warned me that Christmas was one night closer.

Alfie McShane (12)
Royds School, Leeds

Winter's Mysteries

The icy flakes on the ground lay peacefully,
You can hear the enchanting whistle of the wind brushing past your hair.
The snow shimmers like a diamond on the winter snow,
The unending dip of the snow forms a frosty fleece over your feet.
The cold air reaches out and nips my cheek.

Aliesha Chamberlain (12)
Royds School, Leeds

Pure White Snow

I clear my window and look outside
to see a blanket of shining snow, sparkling snow.
My hands are numb, my fingers are nippy
from the frosty, freezing air.
My breath is like ice-cold smoke.
The sun is rising and it is melting the pure white snow.

Joe Dodworth (12)
Royds School, Leeds

Snowy Christmas

The snow was like a coat of fluffiness.
It was my first real Christmas with snow
as smooth as a sheet of crystal glass.
The trees were waving snow at me,
throwing snowy stars into the sky.
Slipping, shivering, sliding.
I made it home.

Marshall George Fodden (12)
Royds School, Leeds

Snow

The white wintry blanket of snow
Was spread around the garden.
It covered my frozen feet
It is like sinking sand.
The snow is soft
Isolating all his surroundings
It lay there glistening.

Katelyn Rowley (12)
Royds School, Leeds

Why Winter Walks Win

Winter walks always win,
The cold, crisp air makes me grin.
The frosted grass
And the frozen droplets,
Make you want to go inside and drink hot chocolate.

Cold wind blows,
Almost freezing my toes!
When, as if out of nowhere,
It begins to snow!

I continue walking
Through the chilly park,
In my fake fur hooded coat
And my adorable little scarf.

My boots clip clop on the icy ground
As I look above me.

What have I found?
An old conker in a tree,
Frosted so perfectly.

Well, I truly believe that winter walks win.
This journey has been absolute bliss,
I'll always reminisce about this!

Nicole Evans (12)
St Illtyd's Catholic High School, Cardiff

Wonderful Winter

Frost is everywhere,
No one's in despair,
The festive season is here,
It's time for laughter and cheer,
It's the middle of December,
The time where we remember,
How wonderful winter is.

There's no blossom to be seen,
Not one of the trees is green,
The ground is a blanket of white,
Outside is a starry night,
It's the middle of December,
The time where we remember,
How wonderful winter is.

Christmas is coming,
Can't wait for the pudding,
The bushes are filled with holly,
And the season is merry and jolly,
It's the middle of December,
The time where we remember,
How wonderful winter is.

Animals scurry away,
So they can play another day,
Christmas jumpers on,
Nothing can go wrong,
It's the middle of December,
The time where we remember,
How wonderful winter is.

Holly Cooper (11)
The Manor Academy, Mansfield

Winter Is Here

The sky is black and the ground is white,
Sitting on the sofa in the cold, cold night.
Cosy pyjamas and fluffy sheets,
Family fun and warm, fuzzy feet.
Relaxed and settled with no bills to pay,
Counting down for Christmas Day.
Fairy lights and magic floating by,
The tasty glorious smell of apple pie.
Constantly getting shivers and shakes,
Building snowmen, no matter how long it takes.
Getting in bed for a good night's sleep,
Waiting for Santa and counting sheep.
Going under blankets as if it was a hut,
Settling down, eyes softly shut.

Mia Green (11)
The Manor Academy, Mansfield

Spelling Out Christmas

C risp snow crunching underfoot,
H uddled together, feeling your touch,
R obins singing festive love,
I cy mornings and snow, white as doves,
S anta Claus, sleigh bells ringing,
T rees with tinsel and church bells dinging.
M ince pies and sweet Christmas cake,
A nd carollers, mulled wine to take.
S easons and feelings you can't destroy,

Christmas fills my life with joy.

Emily Allden (15)
The Manor Academy, Mansfield

Young Writers Information

We hope you have enjoyed reading this book – and that you will continue to in the coming years.

If you're a young adult who enjoys reading and creative writing, or the parent of an enthusiastic poet or story writer, do visit our website **www.youngwriters.co.uk**. Here you will find free competitions, workshops and games, as well as recommended reads, a poetry glossary and our blog.

If you would like to order further copies of this book, or any of our other titles, then please give us a call or visit **www.youngwriters.co.uk**.

Young Writers
Remus House
Coltsfoot Drive
Peterborough
PE2 9BF
(01733) 890066
info@youngwriters.co.uk